Braver in the Saddle: A Rider Confidence & Progress Journal

Emotional support + small wins → Ideal for anxious adult riders, returning riders, or teens.

The Thoughtful Rider Series

Yvonne C Caldwell

Contents

1. Welcome Dear Rider — 1
2. How to Use This Journal — 4
3. When Fear Spikes (What to Do in the Moment) — 9
4. Confidence Anchor Phrases — 15
5. Visualization Before Riding — 21
6. Journal Pages — 26

Chapter 1
Welcome Dear Rider

Yvonne C Caldwell

If this guide journal has found its way into your hands, then you are someone who cares - deeply - about your partnership with your horse. Whether you're returning to riding, rebuilding confidence, or simply wanting to feel a little braver in the saddle, this journal is here to support you.

> Riding takes courage.

Not the flashy kind - but the quiet, steady, "I'll try again today" kind.

This journal is designed to help you notice small wins, reflect kindly on your growth, and celebrate progress - no matter how slow it feels. You'll find space to track your rides, reflect on moments of bravery, and remind yourself that courage can be as simple as showing up.

Take your time.

Write honestly.

Be gentle with yourself.

You are doing better than you think.

Your horse is lucky to have you.

With encouragement,

Yvonne C Caldwell

Braver in the Saddle: A Rider Confidence & Progress Journal

Chapter 2
How to Use This Journal

Braver in the Saddle: A Rider Confidence & Progress Journal

You do **not** need to write every day.

There are no dates printed, so you can use this journal at **your own pace**.

Some weeks you may have many notes.

Some weeks life happens and the journal waits quietly for you.

Both are okay.

The most important goal is to **notice small steps forward**, even when they feel quiet or ordinary.

If you feel stuck then skip ahead.

If you miss a week, just begin again.

There is **no falling behind** in horsemanship or in healing.

How to Use the Different Sections

Two Monthly Mindset Reflection

Use this page once per week, or any time you want to reset, refocus, or check in with how you're feeling.

This is where you notice pride, courage, and growth.

Ride Reflection Pages

Use after each ride, or simply after any moment that felt meaningful.

These pages help you track progress, celebrate wins, and stay kind to yourself while improving.

Monthly Progress Check-In

Use at the end of each month (or every 4–6 weeks).

Stepping back to see the big picture helps you realize how far you've come, often more than you realize.

Support & Confidence Tools in This Journal

These short chapters are here for the moments when riding feels emotional, overwhelming, or uncertain.

When Fear Spikes

Use anytime fear, nerves, or tension appear.

This page offers simple, in-the-moment steps to help your body soften and reconnect with your horse.

Confidence Anchor Phrases

Return to this chapter whenever you need kind, grounding self-talk.

Choose a phrase that helps you breathe easier, not harder.

Visualization Before Riding

Use before mounting, at the barn, or even in the car before your ride.

This helps your mind and body enter the saddle with calm, presence, and softness, not pressure.

You can flip to these pages **whenever needed.**

There is no wrong time to take a moment for yourself.

. . .

One Last Reminder

This guided journal is about:

- Quiet bravery

- Gentle progress

- Your relationship with your horse

You are allowed to go slow, to feel how you feel, and to grow at your own pace.

Take a deep breath and soften your shoulders.

Let's begin.

Yvonne C Caldwell

Chapter 3
When Fear Spikes (What to Do in the Moment)

Fear does not mean you are failing.

It does not mean you are weak, behind, or not meant to ride.

Fear is **information:**

• Something feels new

• Something feels uncertain

• Or something from your past is being reminded by the present

Every rider - every single one - has moments when fear rises unexpectedly.

This chapter gives you **simple, in-the-moment things to do** when your body tenses, your mind races, or your confidence suddenly melts away. These tools help you **stay connected to your horse, soften your body, and return to the moment.**

1. Breathe Low, Not High in Your Chest

When fear appears, breathing changes first, often becoming tight, shallow, or high.

High breathing → signals your nervous system that danger is present.

Low breathing → signals your nervous system that you are safe enough to stay.

Try this:

• Breathe in **through your nose** for 3 slow counts

• Let your belly expand (not your shoulders)

- Breathe out **through your mouth** for 4 - 6 slow counts

You may feel your horse breathe with you, many horses mirror our breath.

2. Look Where You Want to Go

Eyes up = body follows = horse follows.

When we become tense, we often:

- Look down
- Brace
- Freeze
- Or focus on what could go wrong

Gently lift your gaze to:

- The next marker
- The center of the arena
- A soft, far-away point

Your **horse reads your focus** as confidence.

3. Check Your Contact: Soften and Lengthen

Fear often makes riders shorten reins and tighten shoulders, it's automatic.

But short, tight reins can:

- Limit your horse's freedom

- Reduce their ability to move softly
- Increase tension in both of you

Instead:

- Soften your hands
- Lengthen your reins a *small* bit
- Drop your shoulders
- Let your elbows breathe

The message becomes: "I am here with you. We are okay." Your horse feels that.

4. Speak to Yourself with Kindness

Words can shift the nervous system as strongly as breath. Say (out loud if needed):

"I am allowed to take my time."

"I don't have to be perfect to be improving."

These are not motivational slogans, they are **instructions** to your nervous system.

Your horse responds to the rider who is *kind* to themselves, not the rider who demands perfection.

5. Quick Grounding Exercise

Do this slowly, in real time:

1 Pause. You do not need to rush.

2 Feel your seat bones. Let them be heavy and real.

3 Exhale slowly through your mouth. Long exhale = release.

4 Let your horse's walk swing your hips. Allow rhythm to return.

5 Name 3 things you did right today.

(Examples: I showed up. I breathed. I didn't quit.)

These steps gently tell your brain: "I am safe enough to continue."

Remember

Being brave does *not* mean being fearless. It means you are choosing to stay **in the moment**, kindly, one breath at a time.

Yvonne C Caldwell

Chapter 4
Confidence Anchor Phrases

Confidence is not something we *wait* to feel before we ride. It is something we *practice*.

Gently, repeatedly, in small ways.

Often, confidence comes not from pushing harder, but from **speaking to ourselves the way we would speak to a beloved horse.**

With patience.

With encouragement.

With softness.

The phrases on this page are called **Confidence Anchors.**

They help guide your mind back to calm when fear, doubt, or self-pressure begins to build.

You can say them:

- Before mounting

- While grooming

- At the mounting block

- During transitions

- When something feels new or uncertain

- Or simply when you need a moment of grounding

Choose the ones that feel good in your **body**, not just in your mind.

You may only use one and that is enough.

. . .

How to Use Confidence Anchors

1 Breathe in.

2 Say the phrase **slowly**, either aloud or silently.

3 Let your shoulders soften.

4 Feel your horse listening, because they always are.

Repeat as needed. There is no time limit on calm.

Confidence Anchors (Use the ones that help you feel softer, not braver-by-force)

"Progress is progress, even when it's quiet."

You do not need dramatic breakthroughs to be improving. Tiny steps count.

"My horse and I are learning together."

You are not behind. You are a team growing side-by-side.

"I am allowed to take this at my pace."

There is no deadline for confidence. You do not owe speed to anyone.

"Bravery is showing up, not eliminating fear."

You do not need to *feel* fearless to be bold. Just be present.

. . .

Yvonne C Caldwell

"I can breathe and soften, even when I'm unsure."

Uncertainty does not mean stop. It means slow, soften, and stay connected.

Space for Your Personal Anchor Phrases

(Write anything that makes your mind settle and your chest loosen.)

1

2

3

4

You may find new phrases as you ride. Write them down as they come to you.

A Note to You

Your horse does not need you to be fearless. They just need you to be kind, to yourself and to them. Quiet confidence is still confidence. Slow confidence is still confidence. Your confidence is allowed to grow gently. You're already doing the work.

Chapter 5
Visualization Before Riding

Visualization Before Riding

Before you mount, take a moment to arrive, not just physically, but mentally. Horses feel our energy long before they feel our aids.

They notice the quality of our breathing, the softness in our muscles, the steadiness of our focus. Taking a moment to **visualize calm** helps both you and your horse begin the ride with trust and connection.

Visualization is not about imagining perfect movement, flawless transitions, or picture-perfect equitation. It's about creating a moment of *peace*, a quiet space where your mind, body, and horse can meet. You only need 15 to 30 seconds.

Before You Start

Stand near your horse.

Or sit quietly in the barn.

Or simply pause at the mounting block.

There is no wrong time to do this.

Step-by-Step Visualization

1. Close your eyes gently.

No squeezing or forcing, just soft.

2. Notice your horse's breathing.

Feel or imagine the slow rise and fall.

Let your breath follow theirs.

3. Picture the sound of hoof steps.

Steady. Rhythmic. Familiar.

Like a heartbeat outside your body.

4. Imagine your body sitting tall and soft in the saddle.

Tall through your spine.

Soft through your shoulders and hands.

Anchored through your seat.

Breathing.

5. Picture a gentle, connected ride.

Not dramatic.

Not impressive.

Just *harmonious*.

A calm walk.

A quiet circle.

A moment of being together.

Important Reminder

You do **not** need to visualize perfection.

You **do not** need to get every moment right in your mind first.

This practice is not about performance.

It is about presence.

**You are not preparing your horse.

You are preparing your nervous system.**

If Your Mind Wanders

That's okay. That's normal.

Just return to:

- Breath

- Rhythm

- Softness

Let the picture come back slowly, like a horse approaching when you wait quietly.

End the Visualization With:

One gentle exhale.

A softening of your shoulders.

A quiet *"We've got this."*

Then mount with ease, not because you are fearless,

but because you are present.

. . .

A Final Note

Visualization is not pretending. It is remembering who you are when you are calm: A rider who shows up. A rider who cares, and who keeps choosing connection. That is bravery. And you already have it.

Chapter 6
Journal Pages

Weekly Mindset Reflection

Weekly Mindset Reflection

DATE: / /

WHAT MADE ME PROUD THIS WEEK:

_____
_____
_____

WHERE DID I FEEL NERVOUS OR UNSURE?

_____
_____
_____
_____

WHAT HELPED WHEN I FELT ANXIOUS? EVEN A LITTLE BIT?

_____
_____
_____
_____

MY ONE SMALL "BRAVE" GOAL FOR MY NEXT RIDE IS:

_____
_____
_____
_____

Weekly Mindset Reflection

DATE: / /

WHAT MADE ME PROUD TIHIS WEEK:

_____
_____
_____

WHERE DID I FEEL NERVOUS OR UNSURE?

_____
_____
_____
_____
_____

WHAT HELPED WHEN I FELT ANXIOUS? EVEN A LITTLE BIT?

_____
_____
_____
_____
_____

MY ONE SMALL "BRAVE" GOAL FOR MY NEXT RIDE IS:

_____
_____
_____
_____

Weekly Mindset Reflection

DATE: / /

WHAT MADE ME PROUD TIHIS WEEK:

_____
_____
_____

WHERE DID I FEEL NERVOUS OR UNSURE?

_____
_____
_____
_____
_____

WHAT HELPED WHEN I FELT ANXIOUS? EVEN A LITTLE BIT?

_____
_____
_____
_____
_____

MY ONE SMALL "BRAVE" GOAL FOR MY NEXT RIDE IS:

_____
_____
_____
_____
_____

Weekly Mindset Reflection

DATE: / /

WHAT MADE ME PROUD TIHIS WEEK:

_____
_____
_____

WHERE DID I FEEL NERVOUS OR UNSURE?

_____
_____
_____
_____
_____

WHAT HELPED WHEN I FELT ANXIOUS? EVEN A LITTLE BIT?

_____
_____
_____
_____
_____

MY ONE SMALL "BRAVE" GOAL FOR MY NEXT RIDE IS:

_____
_____
_____
_____
_____

Weekly Mindset Reflection

DATE: / /

WHAT MADE ME PROUD THIS WEEK:

_____
_____
_____

WHERE DID I FEEL NERVOUS OR UNSURE?

_____
_____
_____
_____
_____

WHAT HELPED WHEN I FELT ANXIOUS? EVEN A LITTLE BIT?

_____
_____
_____
_____
_____

MY ONE SMALL "BRAVE" GOAL FOR MY NEXT RIDE IS:

_____
_____
_____
_____

Weekly Mindset Reflection

DATE: / /

WHAT MADE ME PROUD TIHIS WEEK:

_____
_____
_____

WHERE DID I FEEL NERVOUS OR UNSURE?

_____
_____
_____
_____

WHAT HELPED WHEN I FELT ANXIOUS? EVEN A LITTLE BIT?

_____
_____
_____
_____

MY ONE SMALL "BRAVE" GOAL FOR MY NEXT RIDE IS:

_____
_____
_____
_____

Weekly Mindset Reflection

DATE: / /

WHAT MADE ME PROUD THIS WEEK:

_____
_____
_____

WHERE DID I FEEL NERVOUS OR UNSURE?

_____
_____
_____
_____
_____

WHAT HELPED WHEN I FELT ANXIOUS? EVEN A LITTLE BIT?

_____
_____
_____
_____
_____

MY ONE SMALL "BRAVE" GOAL FOR MY NEXT RIDE IS:

_____
_____
_____
_____

Weekly Mindset Reflection

DATE: / /

WHAT MADE ME PROUD TIHIS WEEK:

_____
_____
_____

WHERE DID I FEEL NERVOUS OR UNSURE?

_____
_____
_____
_____
_____

WHAT HELPED WHEN I FELT ANXIOUS? EVEN A LITTLE BIT?

_____
_____
_____
_____
_____

MY ONE SMALL "BRAVE" GOAL FOR MY NEXT RIDE IS:

_____
_____
_____
_____
_____

Weekly Mindset Reflection

DATE: / /

WHAT MADE ME PROUD TIHIS WEEK:

_____
_____
_____

WHERE DID I FEEL NERVOUS OR UNSURE?

_____
_____
_____
_____

WHAT HELPED WHEN I FELT ANXIOUS? EVEN A LITTLE BIT?

_____
_____
_____
_____

MY ONE SMALL "BRAVE" GOAL FOR MY NEXT RIDE IS:

_____
_____
_____
_____

Weekly Mindset Reflection

DATE: / /

WHAT MADE ME PROUD TIHIS WEEK:

_____
_____
_____

WHERE DID I FEEL NERVOUS OR UNSURE?

_____
_____
_____
_____
_____

WHAT HELPED WHEN I FELT ANXIOUS? EVEN A LITTLE BIT?

_____
_____
_____
_____
_____

MY ONE SMALL "BRAVE" GOAL FOR MY NEXT RIDE IS:

_____
_____
_____
_____

Weekly Mindset Reflection

DATE: / /

WHAT MADE ME PROUD TIHIS WEEK:

_____
_____
_____

WHERE DID I FEEL NERVOUS OR UNSURE?

_____
_____
_____
_____
_____

WHAT HELPED WHEN I FELT ANXIOUS? EVEN A LITTLE BIT?

_____
_____
_____
_____
_____

MY ONE SMALL "BRAVE" GOAL FOR MY NEXT RIDE IS:

_____
_____
_____
_____
_____

Weekly Mindset Reflection

DATE: / /

WHAT MADE ME PROUD TIHIS WEEK:

_____
_____
_____

WHERE DID I FEEL NERVOUS OR UNSURE?

_____
_____
_____
_____
_____

WHAT HELPED WHEN I FELT ANXIOUS? EVEN A LITTLE BIT?

_____
_____
_____
_____
_____

MY ONE SMALL "BRAVE" GOAL FOR MY NEXT RIDE IS:

_____
_____
_____
_____
_____

Weekly Mindset Reflection

DATE: / /

WHAT MADE ME PROUD TIHIS WEEK:

_____
_____
_____

WHERE DID I FEEL NERVOUS OR UNSURE?

_____
_____
_____
_____
_____

WHAT HELPED WHEN I FELT ANXIOUS? EVEN A LITTLE BIT?

_____
_____
_____
_____
_____

MY ONE SMALL "BRAVE" GOAL FOR MY NEXT RIDE IS:

_____
_____
_____
_____
_____

Weekly Mindset Reflection

DATE: / /

WHAT MADE ME PROUD THIS WEEK:

_____
_____
_____

WHERE DID I FEEL NERVOUS OR UNSURE?

_____
_____
_____
_____
_____

WHAT HELPED WHEN I FELT ANXIOUS? EVEN A LITTLE BIT?

_____
_____
_____
_____
_____

MY ONE SMALL "BRAVE" GOAL FOR MY NEXT RIDE IS:

_____
_____
_____
_____

Weekly Mindset Reflection

DATE: / /

WHAT MADE ME PROUD TIHIS WEEK:

_____
_____
_____

WHERE DID I FEEL NERVOUS OR UNSURE?

_____
_____
_____
_____
_____

WHAT HELPED WHEN I FELT ANXIOUS? EVEN A LITTLE BIT?

_____
_____
_____
_____
_____

MY ONE SMALL "BRAVE" GOAL FOR MY NEXT RIDE IS:

_____
_____
_____
_____
_____

Weekly Mindset Reflection

DATE: / /

WHAT MADE ME PROUD TIHIS WEEK:

_____
_____
_____

WHERE DID I FEEL NERVOUS OR UNSURE?

_____
_____
_____
_____
_____

WHAT HELPED WHEN I FELT ANXIOUS? EVEN A LITTLE BIT?

_____
_____
_____
_____
_____

MY ONE SMALL "BRAVE" GOAL FOR MY NEXT RIDE IS:

_____
_____
_____
_____

Weekly Mindset Reflection

DATE: / /

WHAT MADE ME PROUD TIHIS WEEK:

_____
_____
_____

WHERE DID I FEEL NERVOUS OR UNSURE?

_____
_____
_____
_____
_____

WHAT HELPED WHEN I FELT ANXIOUS? EVEN A LITTLE BIT?

_____
_____
_____
_____
_____

MY ONE SMALL "BRAVE" GOAL FOR MY NEXT RIDE IS:

_____
_____
_____
_____
_____

Weekly Mindset Reflection

DATE: / /

WHAT MADE ME PROUD THIS WEEK:

_____
_____
_____

WHERE DID I FEEL NERVOUS OR UNSURE?

_____
_____
_____
_____
_____

WHAT HELPED WHEN I FELT ANXIOUS? EVEN A LITTLE BIT?

_____
_____
_____
_____
_____

MY ONE SMALL "BRAVE" GOAL FOR MY NEXT RIDE IS:

_____
_____
_____
_____
_____

Weekly Mindset Reflection

DATE: / /

WHAT MADE ME PROUD TIHIS WEEK:

_____
_____
_____

WHERE DID I FEEL NERVOUS OR UNSURE?

_____
_____
_____
_____

WHAT HELPED WHEN I FELT ANXIOUS? EVEN A LITTLE BIT?

_____
_____
_____
_____
_____

MY ONE SMALL "BRAVE" GOAL FOR MY NEXT RIDE IS:

_____
_____
_____
_____
_____

Weekly Mindset Reflection

DATE: / /

WHAT MADE ME PROUD THIS WEEK:

_____
_____
_____

WHERE DID I FEEL NERVOUS OR UNSURE?

_____
_____
_____
_____
_____

WHAT HELPED WHEN I FELT ANXIOUS? EVEN A LITTLE BIT?

_____
_____
_____
_____
_____

MY ONE SMALL "BRAVE" GOAL FOR MY NEXT RIDE IS:

_____
_____
_____
_____

Weekly Mindset Reflection

DATE: / /

WHAT MADE ME PROUD TIHIS WEEK:

_____
_____
_____

WHERE DID I FEEL NERVOUS OR UNSURE?

_____
_____
_____
_____
_____

WHAT HELPED WHEN I FELT ANXIOUS? EVEN A LITTLE BIT?

_____
_____
_____
_____
_____

MY ONE SMALL "BRAVE" GOAL FOR MY NEXT RIDE IS:

_____
_____
_____
_____

Weekly Mindset Reflection

DATE: / /

WHAT MADE ME PROUD TIHIS WEEK:

_____
_____
_____

WHERE DID I FEEL NERVOUS OR UNSURE?

_____
_____
_____
_____
_____

WHAT HELPED WHEN I FELT ANXIOUS? EVEN A LITTLE BIT?

_____
_____
_____
_____
_____

MY ONE SMALL "BRAVE" GOAL FOR MY NEXT RIDE IS:

_____
_____
_____
_____

Weekly Mindset Reflection

DATE: / /

WHAT MADE ME PROUD TIHIS WEEK:

_____
_____
_____

WHERE DID I FEEL NERVOUS OR UNSURE?

_____
_____
_____
_____

WHAT HELPED WHEN I FELT ANXIOUS? EVEN A LITTLE BIT?

_____
_____
_____
_____

MY ONE SMALL "BRAVE" GOAL FOR MY NEXT RIDE IS:

_____
_____
_____
_____

Weekly Mindset Reflection

DATE: / /

WHAT MADE ME PROUD THIS WEEK:

_____
_____
_____

WHERE DID I FEEL NERVOUS OR UNSURE?

_____
_____
_____
_____
_____

WHAT HELPED WHEN I FELT ANXIOUS? EVEN A LITTLE BIT?

_____
_____
_____
_____
_____

MY ONE SMALL "BRAVE" GOAL FOR MY NEXT RIDE IS:

_____
_____
_____
_____

Weekly Mindset Reflection

DATE: / /

WHAT MADE ME PROUD TIHIS WEEK:

_____
_____
_____

WHERE DID I FEEL NERVOUS OR UNSURE?

_____
_____
_____
_____
_____

WHAT HELPED WHEN I FELT ANXIOUS? EVEN A LITTLE BIT?

_____
_____
_____
_____
_____

MY ONE SMALL "BRAVE" GOAL FOR MY NEXT RIDE IS:

_____
_____
_____
_____

Weekly Mindset Reflection

DATE: / /

WHAT MADE ME PROUD TIHIS WEEK:

_____
_____
_____

WHERE DID I FEEL NERVOUS OR UNSURE?

_____
_____
_____
_____
_____

WHAT HELPED WHEN I FELT ANXIOUS? EVEN A LITTLE BIT?

_____
_____
_____
_____
_____

MY ONE SMALL "BRAVE" GOAL FOR MY NEXT RIDE IS:

_____
_____
_____
_____
_____

Weekly Mindset Reflection

DATE: / /

WHAT MADE ME PROUD TIHIS WEEK:

_____
_____
_____

WHERE DID I FEEL NERVOUS OR UNSURE?

_____
_____
_____
_____

WHAT HELPED WHEN I FELT ANXIOUS? EVEN A LITTLE BIT?

_____
_____
_____
_____

MY ONE SMALL "BRAVE" GOAL FOR MY NEXT RIDE IS:

_____
_____
_____

Weekly Mindset Reflection

DATE: / /

WHAT MADE ME PROUD TIHIS WEEK:

_____
_____
_____

WHERE DID I FEEL NERVOUS OR UNSURE?

_____
_____
_____
_____
_____

WHAT HELPED WHEN I FELT ANXIOUS? EVEN A LITTLE BIT?

_____
_____
_____
_____
_____

MY ONE SMALL "BRAVE" GOAL FOR MY NEXT RIDE IS:

_____
_____
_____
_____

Weekly Mindset Reflection

DATE: / /

WHAT MADE ME PROUD TIHIS WEEK:

_____
_____
_____

WHERE DID I FEEL NERVOUS OR UNSURE?

_____
_____
_____
_____
_____

WHAT HELPED WHEN I FELT ANXIOUS? EVEN A LITTLE BIT?

_____
_____
_____
_____
_____

MY ONE SMALL "BRAVE" GOAL FOR MY NEXT RIDE IS:

_____
_____
_____
_____
_____

Weekly Mindset Reflection

DATE: / /

WHAT MADE ME PROUD TIHIS WEEK:

_____
_____
_____

WHERE DID I FEEL NERVOUS OR UNSURE?

_____
_____
_____
_____
_____

WHAT HELPED WHEN I FELT ANXIOUS? EVEN A LITTLE BIT?

_____
_____
_____
_____
_____

MY ONE SMALL "BRAVE" GOAL FOR MY NEXT RIDE IS:

_____
_____
_____
_____
_____

Weekly Mindset Reflection

DATE: / /

WHAT MADE ME PROUD TIHIS WEEK:

_____
_____
_____

WHERE DID I FEEL NERVOUS OR UNSURE?

_____
_____
_____
_____
_____

WHAT HELPED WHEN I FELT ANXIOUS? EVEN A LITTLE BIT?

_____
_____
_____
_____
_____

MY ONE SMALL "BRAVE" GOAL FOR MY NEXT RIDE IS:

_____
_____
_____
_____

Weekly Mindset Reflection

DATE: / /

WHAT MADE ME PROUD THIS WEEK:

_____
_____
_____

WHERE DID I FEEL NERVOUS OR UNSURE?

_____
_____
_____
_____
_____

WHAT HELPED WHEN I FELT ANXIOUS? EVEN A LITTLE BIT?

_____
_____
_____
_____
_____

MY ONE SMALL "BRAVE" GOAL FOR MY NEXT RIDE IS:

_____
_____
_____
_____
_____

Weekly Mindset Reflection

DATE: / /

WHAT MADE ME PROUD THIS WEEK:

_____
_____
_____

WHERE DID I FEEL NERVOUS OR UNSURE?

_____
_____
_____
_____

WHAT HELPED WHEN I FELT ANXIOUS? EVEN A LITTLE BIT?

_____
_____
_____
_____
_____

MY ONE SMALL "BRAVE" GOAL FOR MY NEXT RIDE IS:

_____
_____
_____
_____

Weekly Mindset Reflection

DATE: / /

WHAT MADE ME PROUD TIHIS WEEK:

_____
_____
_____

WHERE DID I FEEL NERVOUS OR UNSURE?

_____
_____
_____
_____

WHAT HELPED WHEN I FELT ANXIOUS? EVEN A LITTLE BIT?

_____
_____
_____
_____

MY ONE SMALL "BRAVE" GOAL FOR MY NEXT RIDE IS:

_____
_____
_____
_____

Weekly Mindset Reflection

DATE: / /

WHAT MADE ME PROUD TIHIS WEEK:

_____
_____
_____

WHERE DID I FEEL NERVOUS OR UNSURE?

_____
_____
_____
_____
_____

WHAT HELPED WHEN I FELT ANXIOUS? EVEN A LITTLE BIT?

_____
_____
_____
_____
_____

MY ONE SMALL "BRAVE" GOAL FOR MY NEXT RIDE IS:

_____
_____
_____
_____

Weekly Mindset Reflection

DATE: / /

WHAT MADE ME PROUD THIS WEEK:

_____
_____
_____

WHERE DID I FEEL NERVOUS OR UNSURE?

_____
_____
_____
_____
_____

WHAT HELPED WHEN I FELT ANXIOUS? EVEN A LITTLE BIT?

_____
_____
_____
_____
_____

MY ONE SMALL "BRAVE" GOAL FOR MY NEXT RIDE IS:

_____
_____
_____
_____

Weekly Mindset Reflection

DATE: / /

WHAT MADE ME PROUD TIHIS WEEK:

_____
_____
_____

WHERE DID I FEEL NERVOUS OR UNSURE?

_____
_____
_____
_____

WHAT HELPED WHEN I FELT ANXIOUS? EVEN A LITTLE BIT?

_____
_____
_____
_____

MY ONE SMALL "BRAVE" GOAL FOR MY NEXT RIDE IS:

_____
_____
_____
_____

Weekly Mindset Reflection

DATE: / /

WHAT MADE ME PROUD THIS WEEK:

_____
_____
_____

WHERE DID I FEEL NERVOUS OR UNSURE?

_____
_____
_____
_____
_____

WHAT HELPED WHEN I FELT ANXIOUS? EVEN A LITTLE BIT?

_____
_____
_____
_____
_____

MY ONE SMALL "BRAVE" GOAL FOR MY NEXT RIDE IS:

_____
_____
_____
_____

Weekly Mindset Reflection

DATE: / /

WHAT MADE ME PROUD TIHIS WEEK:

_____
_____
_____

WHERE DID I FEEL NERVOUS OR UNSURE?

_____
_____
_____
_____
_____

WHAT HELPED WHEN I FELT ANXIOUS? EVEN A LITTLE BIT?

_____
_____
_____
_____
_____

MY ONE SMALL "BRAVE" GOAL FOR MY NEXT RIDE IS:

_____
_____
_____
_____
_____

Weekly Mindset Reflection

DATE: / /

WHAT MADE ME PROUD TIHIS WEEK:

_____
_____
_____

WHERE DID I FEEL NERVOUS OR UNSURE?

_____
_____
_____
_____

WHAT HELPED WHEN I FELT ANXIOUS? EVEN A LITTLE BIT?

_____
_____
_____
_____

MY ONE SMALL "BRAVE" GOAL FOR MY NEXT RIDE IS:

_____
_____
_____
_____

Weekly Mindset Reflection

DATE: / /

WHAT MADE ME PROUD TIHIS WEEK:

_____
_____
_____

WHERE DID I FEEL NERVOUS OR UNSURE?

_____
_____
_____
_____
_____

WHAT HELPED WHEN I FELT ANXIOUS? EVEN A LITTLE BIT?

_____
_____
_____
_____
_____

MY ONE SMALL "BRAVE" GOAL FOR MY NEXT RIDE IS:

_____
_____
_____
_____
_____

Weekly Mindset Reflection

DATE: / /

WHAT MADE ME PROUD THIS WEEK:

_____
_____
_____

WHERE DID I FEEL NERVOUS OR UNSURE?

_____
_____
_____
_____
_____

WHAT HELPED WHEN I FELT ANXIOUS? EVEN A LITTLE BIT?

_____
_____
_____
_____
_____

MY ONE SMALL "BRAVE" GOAL FOR MY NEXT RIDE IS:

_____
_____
_____
_____

Weekly Mindset Reflection

DATE: / /

WHAT MADE ME PROUD TIHIS WEEK:

_____
_____
_____

WHERE DID I FEEL NERVOUS OR UNSURE?

_____
_____
_____
_____
_____

WHAT HELPED WHEN I FELT ANXIOUS? EVEN A LITTLE BIT?

_____
_____
_____
_____
_____

MY ONE SMALL "BRAVE" GOAL FOR MY NEXT RIDE IS:

_____
_____
_____
_____
_____

Weekly Mindset Reflection

DATE: / /

WHAT MADE ME PROUD TIHIS WEEK:

_____
_____
_____

WHERE DID I FEEL NERVOUS OR UNSURE?

_____
_____
_____
_____
_____

WHAT HELPED WHEN I FELT ANXIOUS? EVEN A LITTLE BIT?

_____
_____
_____
_____
_____

MY ONE SMALL "BRAVE" GOAL FOR MY NEXT RIDE IS:

_____
_____
_____
_____
_____

Weekly Mindset Reflection

DATE: / /

WHAT MADE ME PROUD THIS WEEK:

_____
_____
_____

WHERE DID I FEEL NERVOUS OR UNSURE?

_____
_____
_____
_____
_____

WHAT HELPED WHEN I FELT ANXIOUS? EVEN A LITTLE BIT?

_____
_____
_____
_____
_____

MY ONE SMALL "BRAVE" GOAL FOR MY NEXT RIDE IS:

_____
_____
_____
_____

Weekly Mindset Reflection

DATE: / /

WHAT MADE ME PROUD TIHIS WEEK:

_____
_____
_____

WHERE DID I FEEL NERVOUS OR UNSURE?

_____
_____
_____
_____
_____

WHAT HELPED WHEN I FELT ANXIOUS? EVEN A LITTLE BIT?

_____
_____
_____
_____
_____

MY ONE SMALL "BRAVE" GOAL FOR MY NEXT RIDE IS:

_____
_____
_____
_____

Weekly Mindset Reflection

DATE: / /

WHAT MADE ME PROUD TIHIS WEEK:

_____
_____
_____

WHERE DID I FEEL NERVOUS OR UNSURE?

_____
_____
_____
_____
_____

WHAT HELPED WHEN I FELT ANXIOUS? EVEN A LITTLE BIT?

_____
_____
_____
_____
_____

MY ONE SMALL "BRAVE" GOAL FOR MY NEXT RIDE IS:

_____
_____
_____
_____

Weekly Mindset Reflection

DATE: / /

WHAT MADE ME PROUD THIS WEEK:

_____
_____
_____

WHERE DID I FEEL NERVOUS OR UNSURE?

_____
_____
_____
_____
_____

WHAT HELPED WHEN I FELT ANXIOUS? EVEN A LITTLE BIT?

_____
_____
_____
_____
_____

MY ONE SMALL "BRAVE" GOAL FOR MY NEXT RIDE IS:

_____
_____
_____
_____

Weekly Mindset Reflection

DATE: / /

WHAT MADE ME PROUD TIHIS WEEK:

_____
_____
_____

WHERE DID I FEEL NERVOUS OR UNSURE?

_____
_____
_____
_____
_____

WHAT HELPED WHEN I FELT ANXIOUS? EVEN A LITTLE BIT?

_____
_____
_____
_____
_____

MY ONE SMALL "BRAVE" GOAL FOR MY NEXT RIDE IS:

_____
_____
_____
_____

Weekly Mindset Reflection

DATE: / /

WHAT MADE ME PROUD THIS WEEK:

_____
_____
_____

WHERE DID I FEEL NERVOUS OR UNSURE?

_____
_____
_____
_____
_____

WHAT HELPED WHEN I FELT ANXIOUS? EVEN A LITTLE BIT?

_____
_____
_____
_____
_____

MY ONE SMALL "BRAVE" GOAL FOR MY NEXT RIDE IS:

_____
_____
_____
_____
_____

Weekly Mindset Reflection

DATE: / /

WHAT MADE ME PROUD THIS WEEK:

_____
_____
_____

WHERE DID I FEEL NERVOUS OR UNSURE?

_____
_____
_____
_____
_____

WHAT HELPED WHEN I FELT ANXIOUS? EVEN A LITTLE BIT?

_____
_____
_____
_____
_____

MY ONE SMALL "BRAVE" GOAL FOR MY NEXT RIDE IS:

_____
_____
_____
_____

Weekly Mindset Reflection

DATE: / /

WHAT MADE ME PROUD THIS WEEK:

_____
_____
_____

WHERE DID I FEEL NERVOUS OR UNSURE?

_____
_____
_____
_____
_____

WHAT HELPED WHEN I FELT ANXIOUS? EVEN A LITTLE BIT?

_____
_____
_____
_____
_____

MY ONE SMALL "BRAVE" GOAL FOR MY NEXT RIDE IS:

_____
_____
_____
_____

Ride Reflection

Ride Reflection

DATE: / /

HORSE: _____

HOW I FELT AT THE START (CIRCLE ONE)

1   2   3   4   5

1 (Very Anxious / Unsure)   5 (Calm & Confident)

TODAYS FOCUS:
_____
_____

SMALL WINS FROM TODAY? .
_____
_____
_____

SOMETHING I'D LIKE TO GROW/PRACTISE
_____
_____
_____
_____

HOW I FELT AT THE END (CIRCLE ONE)

1   2   3   4   5

A KIND NOTE TO MYSELF
_____
_____
_____

Ride Reflection

DATE: / /

HORSE: _____

HOW I FELT AT THE START (CIRCLE ONE)

1   2   3   4   5

1 (Very Anxious / Unsure)   5 (Calm & Confident)

TODAYS FOCUS:
_____
_____

SMALL WINS FROM TODAY? .
_____
_____
_____

SOMETHING I'D LIKE TO GROW/PRACTISE
_____
_____
_____
_____

HOW I FELT AT THE END (CIRCLE ONE)

1   2   3   4   5

A KIND NOTE TO MYSELF
_____
_____
_____

Ride Reflection

DATE: / /
HORSE:_____

HOW I FELT AT THE START (CIRCLE ONE)

1   2   3   4   5

1 (Very Anxious / Unsure)   5 (Calm & Confident)

TODAYS FOCUS:
_____
_____

SMALL WINS FROM TODAY?   .
_____
_____
_____

SOMETHING I'D LIKE TO GROW/PRACTISE
_____
_____
_____
_____

HOW I FELT AT THE END (CIRCLE ONE)

1   2   3   4   5

A KIND NOTE TO MYSELF
_____
_____
_____

Ride Reflection

DATE: / /
HORSE:_____

HOW I FELT AT THE START (CIRCLE ONE)

1   2   3   4   5

1 (Very Anxious / Unsure)   5 (Calm & Confident)

TODAYS FOCUS:
_____
_____

SMALL WINS FROM TODAY?   .
_____
_____
_____

SOMETHING I'D LIKE TO GROW/PRACTISE
_____
_____
_____
_____

HOW I FELT AT THE END (CIRCLE ONE)

1   2   3   4   5

A KIND NOTE TO MYSELF
_____
_____
_____

Ride Reflection

DATE: / /

HORSE: _____

HOW I FELT AT THE START (CIRCLE ONE)

1   2   3   4   5

1 (Very Anxious / Unsure)   5 (Calm & Confident)

TODAYS FOCUS:

_____
_____

SMALL WINS FROM TODAY? .

_____
_____
_____

SOMETHING I'D LIKE TO GROW/PRACTISE

_____
_____
_____
_____

HOW I FELT AT THE END (CIRCLE ONE)

1   2   3   4   5

A KIND NOTE TO MYSELF

_____
_____
_____

Ride Reflection

DATE: / /

HORSE: _____

HOW I FELT AT THE START (CIRCLE ONE)

1   2   3   4   5

1 (Very Anxious / Unsure)   5 (Calm & Confident)

TODAYS FOCUS:

_____
_____

SMALL WINS FROM TODAY? .

_____
_____
_____

SOMETHING I'D LIKE TO GROW/PRACTISE

_____
_____
_____
_____

HOW I FELT AT THE END (CIRCLE ONE)

1   2   3   4   5

A KIND NOTE TO MYSELF

_____
_____
_____

Ride Reflection

DATE: / /

HORSE: _____

HOW I FELT AT THE START (CIRCLE ONE)

1   2   3   4   5

1 (Very Anxious / Unsure)   5 (Calm & Confident)

TODAYS FOCUS:

_____
_____

SMALL WINS FROM TODAY? .

_____
_____
_____

SOMETHING I'D LIKE TO GROW/PRACTISE

_____
_____
_____
_____
_____

HOW I FELT AT THE END (CIRCLE ONE)

1   2   3   4   5

A KIND NOTE TO MYSELF

_____
_____
_____

Ride Reflection

DATE: / /

HORSE: _____

HOW I FELT AT THE START (CIRCLE ONE)

1   2   3   4   5

1 (Very Anxious / Unsure)   5 (Calm & Confident)

TODAYS FOCUS:

_____
_____

SMALL WINS FROM TODAY? .

_____
_____
_____

SOMETHING I'D LIKE TO GROW/PRACTISE

_____
_____
_____
_____
_____

HOW I FELT AT THE END (CIRCLE ONE)

1   2   3   4   5

A KIND NOTE TO MYSELF

_____
_____
_____

Ride Reflection

DATE: / /

HORSE: _____

HOW I FELT AT THE START (CIRCLE ONE)

1   2   3   4   5

1 (Very Anxious / Unsure)   5 (Calm & Confident)

TODAYS FOCUS:
_____
_____

SMALL WINS FROM TODAY? .
_____
_____
_____

SOMETHING I'D LIKE TO GROW/PRACTISE
_____
_____
_____
_____

HOW I FELT AT THE END (CIRCLE ONE)

1   2   3   4   5

A KIND NOTE TO MYSELF
_____
_____
_____

Ride Reflection

DATE: / /

HORSE: _____

HOW I FELT AT THE START (CIRCLE ONE)

1   2   3   4   5

1 (Very Anxious / Unsure)   5 (Calm & Confident)

TODAYS FOCUS:
_____
_____

SMALL WINS FROM TODAY? .
_____
_____
_____

SOMETHING I'D LIKE TO GROW/PRACTISE
_____
_____
_____
_____

HOW I FELT AT THE END (CIRCLE ONE)

1   2   3   4   5

A KIND NOTE TO MYSELF
_____
_____
_____

Ride Reflection

DATE: / /

HORSE: _____

HOW I FELT AT THE START (CIRCLE ONE)

1   2   3   4   5

1 (Very Anxious / Unsure)   5 (Calm & Confident)

TODAYS FOCUS:
_____
_____

SMALL WINS FROM TODAY? .
_____
_____
_____

SOMETHING I'D LIKE TO GROW/PRACTISE
_____
_____
_____
_____

HOW I FELT AT THE END (CIRCLE ONE)

1   2   3   4   5

A KIND NOTE TO MYSELF
_____
_____
_____

Ride Reflection

DATE: / /

HORSE: _____

HOW I FELT AT THE START (CIRCLE ONE)

1   2   3   4   5

1 (Very Anxious / Unsure)   5 (Calm & Confident)

TODAYS FOCUS:
_____
_____

SMALL WINS FROM TODAY? .
_____
_____
_____

SOMETHING I'D LIKE TO GROW/PRACTISE
_____
_____
_____
_____

HOW I FELT AT THE END (CIRCLE ONE)

1   2   3   4   5

A KIND NOTE TO MYSELF
_____
_____
_____

Ride Reflection

DATE: / /
HORSE: _____

HOW I FELT AT THE START (CIRCLE ONE)

1   2   3   4   5

1 (Very Anxious / Unsure)   5 (Calm & Confident)

TODAYS FOCUS:
_____
_____

SMALL WINS FROM TODAY?   .
_____
_____
_____

SOMETHING I'D LIKE TO GROW/PRACTISE
_____
_____
_____
_____

HOW I FELT AT THE END (CIRCLE ONE)

1   2   3   4   5

A KIND NOTE TO MYSELF
_____
_____
_____

Ride Reflection

DATE: / /
HORSE: _____

HOW I FELT AT THE START (CIRCLE ONE)

1   2   3   4   5

1 (Very Anxious / Unsure)   5 (Calm & Confident)

TODAYS FOCUS:
_____
_____

SMALL WINS FROM TODAY?   .
_____
_____
_____

SOMETHING I'D LIKE TO GROW/PRACTISE
_____
_____
_____
_____

HOW I FELT AT THE END (CIRCLE ONE)

1   2   3   4   5

A KIND NOTE TO MYSELF
_____
_____
_____

Ride Reflection

DATE: / /

HORSE: _____

HOW I FELT AT THE START (CIRCLE ONE)

1   2   3   4   5

1 (Very Anxious / Unsure)   5 (Calm & Confident)

TODAYS FOCUS:
_____
_____

SMALL WINS FROM TODAY? .
_____
_____
_____

SOMETHING I'D LIKE TO GROW/PRACTISE
_____
_____
_____
_____

HOW I FELT AT THE END (CIRCLE ONE)

1   2   3   4   5

A KIND NOTE TO MYSELF
_____
_____
_____

Ride Reflection

DATE: / /

HORSE: _____

HOW I FELT AT THE START (CIRCLE ONE)

1   2   3   4   5

1 (Very Anxious / Unsure)   5 (Calm & Confident)

TODAYS FOCUS:
_____
_____

SMALL WINS FROM TODAY? .
_____
_____
_____

SOMETHING I'D LIKE TO GROW/PRACTISE
_____
_____
_____
_____

HOW I FELT AT THE END (CIRCLE ONE)

1   2   3   4   5

A KIND NOTE TO MYSELF
_____
_____
_____

Ride Reflection

DATE: / /

HORSE: _____

HOW I FELT AT THE START (CIRCLE ONE)

1   2   3   4   5

1 (Very Anxious / Unsure)   5 (Calm & Confident)

TODAYS FOCUS:

_____
_____

SMALL WINS FROM TODAY?   .

_____
_____
_____

SOMETHING I'D LIKE TO GROW/PRACTISE

_____
_____
_____
_____

HOW I FELT AT THE END (CIRCLE ONE)

1   2   3   4   5

A KIND NOTE TO MYSELF

_____
_____
_____

Ride Reflection

DATE: / /

HORSE: _____

HOW I FELT AT THE START (CIRCLE ONE)

1   2   3   4   5

1 (Very Anxious / Unsure)   5 (Calm & Confident)

TODAYS FOCUS:

_____
_____

SMALL WINS FROM TODAY?   .

_____
_____
_____

SOMETHING I'D LIKE TO GROW/PRACTISE

_____
_____
_____
_____

HOW I FELT AT THE END (CIRCLE ONE)

1   2   3   4   5

A KIND NOTE TO MYSELF

_____
_____
_____

Ride Reflection

DATE: / /

HORSE: _____

HOW I FELT AT THE START (CIRCLE ONE)

1 2 3 4 5

1 (Very Anxious / Unsure)   5 (Calm & Confident)

TODAYS FOCUS:

_____
_____

SMALL WINS FROM TODAY? .

_____
_____
_____

SOMETHING I'D LIKE TO GROW/PRACTISE

_____
_____
_____
_____
_____

HOW I FELT AT THE END (CIRCLE ONE)

1 2 3 4 5

A KIND NOTE TO MYSELF

_____
_____
_____

Ride Reflection

DATE: / /

HORSE: _____

HOW I FELT AT THE START (CIRCLE ONE)

1 2 3 4 5

1 (Very Anxious / Unsure)   5 (Calm & Confident)

TODAYS FOCUS:

_____
_____

SMALL WINS FROM TODAY? .

_____
_____
_____

SOMETHING I'D LIKE TO GROW/PRACTISE

_____
_____
_____
_____
_____

HOW I FELT AT THE END (CIRCLE ONE)

1 2 3 4 5

A KIND NOTE TO MYSELF

_____
_____
_____

Ride Reflection

DATE: / /
HORSE: _____

HOW I FELT AT THE START (CIRCLE ONE)

1   2   3   4   5

1 (Very Anxious / Unsure)   5 (Calm & Confident)

TODAYS FOCUS:
_____
_____

SMALL WINS FROM TODAY? .
_____
_____
_____

SOMETHING I'D LIKE TO GROW/PRACTISE
_____
_____
_____
_____

HOW I FELT AT THE END (CIRCLE ONE)

1   2   3   4   5

A KIND NOTE TO MYSELF
_____
_____
_____

Ride Reflection

DATE: / /
HORSE: _____

HOW I FELT AT THE START (CIRCLE ONE)

1   2   3   4   5

1 (Very Anxious / Unsure)   5 (Calm & Confident)

TODAYS FOCUS:
_____
_____

SMALL WINS FROM TODAY? .
_____
_____
_____

SOMETHING I'D LIKE TO GROW/PRACTISE
_____
_____
_____
_____

HOW I FELT AT THE END (CIRCLE ONE)

1   2   3   4   5

A KIND NOTE TO MYSELF
_____
_____
_____

Ride Reflection

DATE: / /

HORSE: _____

HOW I FELT AT THE START (CIRCLE ONE)

1   2   3   4   5

1 (Very Anxious / Unsure)   5 (Calm & Confident)

TODAYS FOCUS:
_____
_____

SMALL WINS FROM TODAY? .
_____
_____
_____

SOMETHING I'D LIKE TO GROW/PRACTISE
_____
_____
_____
_____

HOW I FELT AT THE END (CIRCLE ONE)

1   2   3   4   5

A KIND NOTE TO MYSELF
_____
_____
_____

Ride Reflection

DATE: / /

HORSE: _____

HOW I FELT AT THE START (CIRCLE ONE)

1   2   3   4   5

1 (Very Anxious / Unsure)   5 (Calm & Confident)

TODAYS FOCUS:
_____
_____

SMALL WINS FROM TODAY? .
_____
_____
_____

SOMETHING I'D LIKE TO GROW/PRACTISE
_____
_____
_____
_____

HOW I FELT AT THE END (CIRCLE ONE)

1   2   3   4   5

A KIND NOTE TO MYSELF
_____
_____
_____

Ride Reflection

DATE: / /

HORSE: _____

HOW I FELT AT THE START (CIRCLE ONE)

1   2   3   4   5

1 (Very Anxious / Unsure)   5 (Calm & Confident)

TODAYS FOCUS:
_____
_____

SMALL WINS FROM TODAY?
_____
_____
_____

SOMETHING I'D LIKE TO GROW/PRACTISE
_____
_____
_____
_____

HOW I FELT AT THE END (CIRCLE ONE)

1   2   3   4   5

A KIND NOTE TO MYSELF
_____
_____
_____

Ride Reflection

DATE: / /

HORSE: _____

HOW I FELT AT THE START (CIRCLE ONE)

1   2   3   4   5

1 (Very Anxious / Unsure)   5 (Calm & Confident)

TODAYS FOCUS:
_____
_____

SMALL WINS FROM TODAY?
_____
_____
_____

SOMETHING I'D LIKE TO GROW/PRACTISE
_____
_____
_____
_____

HOW I FELT AT THE END (CIRCLE ONE)

1   2   3   4   5

A KIND NOTE TO MYSELF
_____
_____
_____

Ride Reflection

DATE: / /

HORSE: _____

HOW I FELT AT THE START (CIRCLE ONE)

1   2   3   4   5

1 (Very Anxious / Unsure)   5 (Calm & Confident)

TODAYS FOCUS:
_____
_____

SMALL WINS FROM TODAY? .
_____
_____
_____

SOMETHING I'D LIKE TO GROW/PRACTISE
_____
_____
_____
_____

HOW I FELT AT THE END (CIRCLE ONE)

1   2   3   4   5

A KIND NOTE TO MYSELF
_____
_____
_____

Ride Reflection

DATE: / /

HORSE: _____

HOW I FELT AT THE START (CIRCLE ONE)

1   2   3   4   5

1 (Very Anxious / Unsure)   5 (Calm & Confident)

TODAYS FOCUS:
_____
_____

SMALL WINS FROM TODAY? .
_____
_____
_____

SOMETHING I'D LIKE TO GROW/PRACTISE
_____
_____
_____
_____

HOW I FELT AT THE END (CIRCLE ONE)

1   2   3   4   5

A KIND NOTE TO MYSELF
_____
_____
_____

Ride Reflection

DATE: / /

HORSE: _____

HOW I FELT AT THE START (CIRCLE ONE)

1   2   3   4   5

1 (Very Anxious / Unsure)   5 (Calm & Confident)

TODAYS FOCUS:
_____
_____

SMALL WINS FROM TODAY?   .
_____
_____
_____

SOMETHING I'D LIKE TO GROW/PRACTISE
_____
_____
_____
_____

HOW I FELT AT THE END (CIRCLE ONE)

1   2   3   4   5

A KIND NOTE TO MYSELF
_____
_____
_____

Ride Reflection

DATE: / /

HORSE: _____

HOW I FELT AT THE START (CIRCLE ONE)

1   2   3   4   5

1 (Very Anxious / Unsure)   5 (Calm & Confident)

TODAYS FOCUS:
_____
_____

SMALL WINS FROM TODAY?   .
_____
_____
_____

SOMETHING I'D LIKE TO GROW/PRACTISE
_____
_____
_____
_____

HOW I FELT AT THE END (CIRCLE ONE)

1   2   3   4   5

A KIND NOTE TO MYSELF
_____
_____
_____

Ride Reflection

DATE: / /

HORSE: _____

HOW I FELT AT THE START (CIRCLE ONE)

1   2   3   4   5

1 (Very Anxious / Unsure)   5 (Calm & Confident)

TODAYS FOCUS:

_____
_____

SMALL WINS FROM TODAY?   .

_____
_____
_____

SOMETHING I'D LIKE TO GROW/PRACTISE

_____
_____
_____
_____

HOW I FELT AT THE END (CIRCLE ONE)

1   2   3   4   5

A KIND NOTE TO MYSELF

_____
_____
_____

Ride Reflection

DATE: / /

HORSE: _____

HOW I FELT AT THE START (CIRCLE ONE)

1   2   3   4   5

1 (Very Anxious / Unsure)   5 (Calm & Confident)

TODAYS FOCUS:

_____
_____

SMALL WINS FROM TODAY?   .

_____
_____
_____

SOMETHING I'D LIKE TO GROW/PRACTISE

_____
_____
_____
_____

HOW I FELT AT THE END (CIRCLE ONE)

1   2   3   4   5

A KIND NOTE TO MYSELF

_____
_____
_____

Ride Reflection

DATE: / /

HORSE: _____

HOW I FELT AT THE START (CIRCLE ONE)

1   2   3   4   5

1 (Very Anxious / Unsure)   5 (Calm & Confident)

TODAYS FOCUS:
_____
_____

SMALL WINS FROM TODAY? .
_____
_____
_____

SOMETHING I'D LIKE TO GROW/PRACTISE
_____
_____
_____
_____

HOW I FELT AT THE END (CIRCLE ONE)

1   2   3   4   5

A KIND NOTE TO MYSELF
_____
_____
_____

Ride Reflection

DATE: / /

HORSE: _____

HOW I FELT AT THE START (CIRCLE ONE)

1   2   3   4   5

1 (Very Anxious / Unsure)   5 (Calm & Confident)

TODAYS FOCUS:
_____
_____

SMALL WINS FROM TODAY? .
_____
_____
_____

SOMETHING I'D LIKE TO GROW/PRACTISE
_____
_____
_____
_____

HOW I FELT AT THE END (CIRCLE ONE)

1   2   3   4   5

A KIND NOTE TO MYSELF
_____
_____
_____

Ride Reflection

DATE: / /

HORSE: _____

HOW I FELT AT THE START (CIRCLE ONE)

1   2   3   4   5

1 (Very Anxious / Unsure)   5 (Calm & Confident)

TODAYS FOCUS:
_____
_____

SMALL WINS FROM TODAY? .
_____
_____
_____

SOMETHING I'D LIKE TO GROW/PRACTISE
_____
_____
_____
_____

HOW I FELT AT THE END (CIRCLE ONE)

1   2   3   4   5

A KIND NOTE TO MYSELF
_____
_____
_____

Ride Reflection

DATE: / /

HORSE: _____

HOW I FELT AT THE START (CIRCLE ONE)

1   2   3   4   5

1 (Very Anxious / Unsure)   5 (Calm & Confident)

TODAYS FOCUS:
_____
_____

SMALL WINS FROM TODAY? .
_____
_____
_____

SOMETHING I'D LIKE TO GROW/PRACTISE
_____
_____
_____
_____

HOW I FELT AT THE END (CIRCLE ONE)

1   2   3   4   5

A KIND NOTE TO MYSELF
_____
_____
_____

Ride Reflection

DATE: / /

HORSE: _____

HOW I FELT AT THE START (CIRCLE ONE)

1   2   3   4   5

1 (Very Anxious / Unsure)   5 (Calm & Confident)

TODAYS FOCUS:
_____
_____

SMALL WINS FROM TODAY? .
_____
_____
_____

SOMETHING I'D LIKE TO GROW/PRACTISE
_____
_____
_____
_____

HOW I FELT AT THE END (CIRCLE ONE)

1   2   3   4   5

A KIND NOTE TO MYSELF
_____
_____
_____

Ride Reflection

DATE: / /

HORSE: _____

HOW I FELT AT THE START (CIRCLE ONE)

1   2   3   4   5

1 (Very Anxious / Unsure)   5 (Calm & Confident)

TODAYS FOCUS:
_____
_____

SMALL WINS FROM TODAY? .
_____
_____
_____

SOMETHING I'D LIKE TO GROW/PRACTISE
_____
_____
_____
_____

HOW I FELT AT THE END (CIRCLE ONE)

1   2   3   4   5

A KIND NOTE TO MYSELF
_____
_____
_____

Ride Reflection

DATE: / /

HORSE: _____

HOW I FELT AT THE START (CIRCLE ONE)

1   2   3   4   5

1 (Very Anxious / Unsure)   5 (Calm & Confident)

TODAYS FOCUS:

_____
_____

SMALL WINS FROM TODAY?   .

_____
_____
_____

SOMETHING I'D LIKE TO GROW/PRACTISE

_____
_____
_____
_____

HOW I FELT AT THE END (CIRCLE ONE)

1   2   3   4   5

A KIND NOTE TO MYSELF

_____
_____
_____

Ride Reflection

DATE: / /

HORSE: _____

HOW I FELT AT THE START (CIRCLE ONE)

1   2   3   4   5

1 (Very Anxious / Unsure)   5 (Calm & Confident)

TODAYS FOCUS:

_____
_____

SMALL WINS FROM TODAY?   .

_____
_____
_____

SOMETHING I'D LIKE TO GROW/PRACTISE

_____
_____
_____
_____

HOW I FELT AT THE END (CIRCLE ONE)

1   2   3   4   5

A KIND NOTE TO MYSELF

_____
_____
_____

Ride Reflection

DATE: / /

HORSE: _____

HOW I FELT AT THE START (CIRCLE ONE)

1   2   3   4   5

1 (Very Anxious / Unsure)   5 (Calm & Confident)

TODAYS FOCUS:

_____
_____

SMALL WINS FROM TODAY? .

_____
_____
_____

SOMETHING I'D LIKE TO GROW/PRACTISE

_____
_____
_____
_____

HOW I FELT AT THE END (CIRCLE ONE)

1   2   3   4   5

A KIND NOTE TO MYSELF

_____
_____
_____

Ride Reflection

DATE: / /

HORSE: _____

HOW I FELT AT THE START (CIRCLE ONE)

1   2   3   4   5

1 (Very Anxious / Unsure)   5 (Calm & Confident)

TODAYS FOCUS:

_____
_____

SMALL WINS FROM TODAY? .

_____
_____
_____

SOMETHING I'D LIKE TO GROW/PRACTISE

_____
_____
_____
_____

HOW I FELT AT THE END (CIRCLE ONE)

1   2   3   4   5

A KIND NOTE TO MYSELF

_____
_____
_____

Ride Reflection

DATE: / /
HORSE: _____

HOW I FELT AT THE START (CIRCLE ONE)

1   2   3   4   5

1 (Very Anxious / Unsure)   5 (Calm & Confident)

TODAYS FOCUS:
_____
_____

SMALL WINS FROM TODAY?   .
_____
_____
_____

SOMETHING I'D LIKE TO GROW/PRACTISE
_____
_____
_____
_____
_____

HOW I FELT AT THE END (CIRCLE ONE)

1   2   3   4   5

A KIND NOTE TO MYSELF
_____
_____
_____

Ride Reflection

DATE: / /
HORSE: _____

HOW I FELT AT THE START (CIRCLE ONE)

1   2   3   4   5

1 (Very Anxious / Unsure)   5 (Calm & Confident)

TODAYS FOCUS:
_____
_____

SMALL WINS FROM TODAY?   .
_____
_____
_____

SOMETHING I'D LIKE TO GROW/PRACTISE
_____
_____
_____
_____
_____

HOW I FELT AT THE END (CIRCLE ONE)

1   2   3   4   5

A KIND NOTE TO MYSELF
_____
_____
_____

Ride Reflection

DATE: / /

HORSE: _____

HOW I FELT AT THE START (CIRCLE ONE)

1   2   3   4   5

1 (Very Anxious / Unsure)   5 (Calm & Confident)

TODAYS FOCUS:

_____
_____

SMALL WINS FROM TODAY? .

_____
_____
_____

SOMETHING I'D LIKE TO GROW/PRACTISE

_____
_____
_____
_____

HOW I FELT AT THE END (CIRCLE ONE)

1   2   3   4   5

A KIND NOTE TO MYSELF

_____
_____
_____

Ride Reflection

DATE: / /

HORSE: _____

HOW I FELT AT THE START (CIRCLE ONE)

1   2   3   4   5

1 (Very Anxious / Unsure)   5 (Calm & Confident)

TODAYS FOCUS:

_____
_____

SMALL WINS FROM TODAY? .

_____
_____
_____

SOMETHING I'D LIKE TO GROW/PRACTISE

_____
_____
_____
_____

HOW I FELT AT THE END (CIRCLE ONE)

1   2   3   4   5

A KIND NOTE TO MYSELF

_____
_____
_____

Ride Reflection

DATE: / /

HORSE: _____

HOW I FELT AT THE START (CIRCLE ONE)

1   2   3   4   5

1 (Very Anxious / Unsure)   5 (Calm & Confident)

TODAYS FOCUS:
_____
_____

SMALL WINS FROM TODAY?   .
_____
_____
_____

SOMETHING I'D LIKE TO GROW/PRACTISE
_____
_____
_____
_____
_____

HOW I FELT AT THE END (CIRCLE ONE)

1   2   3   4   5

A KIND NOTE TO MYSELF
_____
_____
_____

Ride Reflection

DATE: / /

HORSE: _____

HOW I FELT AT THE START (CIRCLE ONE)

1   2   3   4   5

1 (Very Anxious / Unsure)   5 (Calm & Confident)

TODAYS FOCUS:
_____
_____

SMALL WINS FROM TODAY?   .
_____
_____
_____

SOMETHING I'D LIKE TO GROW/PRACTISE
_____
_____
_____
_____
_____

HOW I FELT AT THE END (CIRCLE ONE)

1   2   3   4   5

A KIND NOTE TO MYSELF
_____
_____
_____

Ride Reflection

DATE: / /

HORSE: _____

HOW I FELT AT THE START (CIRCLE ONE)

1   2   3   4   5

1 (Very Anxious / Unsure)   5 (Calm & Confident)

TODAYS FOCUS:
_____
_____

SMALL WINS FROM TODAY?
_____
_____
_____

SOMETHING I'D LIKE TO GROW/PRACTISE
_____
_____
_____
_____

HOW I FELT AT THE END (CIRCLE ONE)

1   2   3   4   5

A KIND NOTE TO MYSELF
_____
_____
_____

Ride Reflection

DATE: / /

HORSE: _____

HOW I FELT AT THE START (CIRCLE ONE)

1   2   3   4   5

1 (Very Anxious / Unsure)   5 (Calm & Confident)

TODAYS FOCUS:
_____
_____

SMALL WINS FROM TODAY?
_____
_____
_____

SOMETHING I'D LIKE TO GROW/PRACTISE
_____
_____
_____
_____

HOW I FELT AT THE END (CIRCLE ONE)

1   2   3   4   5

A KIND NOTE TO MYSELF
_____
_____
_____

Ride Reflection

DATE: / /

HORSE: _____

HOW I FELT AT THE START (CIRCLE ONE)

1   2   3   4   5

1 (Very Anxious / Unsure)   5 (Calm & Confident)

TODAYS FOCUS:
_____
_____

SMALL WINS FROM TODAY? .
_____
_____
_____

SOMETHING I'D LIKE TO GROW/PRACTISE
_____
_____
_____
_____

HOW I FELT AT THE END (CIRCLE ONE)

1   2   3   4   5

A KIND NOTE TO MYSELF
_____
_____
_____

Ride Reflection

DATE: / /

HORSE: _____

HOW I FELT AT THE START (CIRCLE ONE)

1   2   3   4   5

1 (Very Anxious / Unsure)   5 (Calm & Confident)

TODAYS FOCUS:
_____
_____

SMALL WINS FROM TODAY? .
_____
_____
_____

SOMETHING I'D LIKE TO GROW/PRACTISE
_____
_____
_____
_____

HOW I FELT AT THE END (CIRCLE ONE)

1   2   3   4   5

A KIND NOTE TO MYSELF
_____
_____
_____

Ride Reflection

DATE: / /

HORSE: _____

HOW I FELT AT THE START (CIRCLE ONE)

1   2   3   4   5

1 (Very Anxious / Unsure)   5 (Calm & Confident)

TODAYS FOCUS:
_____
_____

SMALL WINS FROM TODAY? .
_____
_____
_____

SOMETHING I'D LIKE TO GROW/PRACTISE
_____
_____
_____
_____

HOW I FELT AT THE END (CIRCLE ONE)

1   2   3   4   5

A KIND NOTE TO MYSELF
_____
_____
_____

Ride Reflection

DATE: / /

HORSE: _____

HOW I FELT AT THE START (CIRCLE ONE)

1   2   3   4   5

1 (Very Anxious / Unsure)   5 (Calm & Confident)

TODAYS FOCUS:
_____
_____

SMALL WINS FROM TODAY? .
_____
_____
_____

SOMETHING I'D LIKE TO GROW/PRACTISE
_____
_____
_____
_____

HOW I FELT AT THE END (CIRCLE ONE)

1   2   3   4   5

A KIND NOTE TO MYSELF
_____
_____
_____

Ride Reflection

DATE: / /

HORSE: _____

HOW I FELT AT THE START (CIRCLE ONE)

1   2   3   4   5

1 (Very Anxious / Unsure)   5 (Calm & Confident)

TODAYS FOCUS:
_____
_____

SMALL WINS FROM TODAY? .
_____
_____
_____

SOMETHING I'D LIKE TO GROW/PRACTISE
_____
_____
_____
_____

HOW I FELT AT THE END (CIRCLE ONE)

1   2   3   4   5

A KIND NOTE TO MYSELF
_____
_____
_____

Ride Reflection

DATE: / /

HORSE: _____

HOW I FELT AT THE START (CIRCLE ONE)

1   2   3   4   5

1 (Very Anxious / Unsure)   5 (Calm & Confident)

TODAYS FOCUS:
_____
_____

SMALL WINS FROM TODAY? .
_____
_____
_____

SOMETHING I'D LIKE TO GROW/PRACTISE
_____
_____
_____
_____

HOW I FELT AT THE END (CIRCLE ONE)

1   2   3   4   5

A KIND NOTE TO MYSELF
_____
_____
_____

Ride Reflection

DATE: / /

HORSE: _____

HOW I FELT AT THE START (CIRCLE ONE)

1   2   3   4   5

1 (Very Anxious / Unsure)   5 (Calm & Confident)

TODAYS FOCUS:

_____
_____

SMALL WINS FROM TODAY? .

_____
_____
_____

SOMETHING I'D LIKE TO GROW/PRACTISE

_____
_____
_____
_____

HOW I FELT AT THE END (CIRCLE ONE)

1   2   3   4   5

A KIND NOTE TO MYSELF

_____
_____
_____

Ride Reflection

DATE: / /

HORSE: _____

HOW I FELT AT THE START (CIRCLE ONE)

1   2   3   4   5

1 (Very Anxious / Unsure)   5 (Calm & Confident)

TODAYS FOCUS:

_____
_____

SMALL WINS FROM TODAY? .

_____
_____
_____

SOMETHING I'D LIKE TO GROW/PRACTISE

_____
_____
_____
_____

HOW I FELT AT THE END (CIRCLE ONE)

1   2   3   4   5

A KIND NOTE TO MYSELF

_____
_____
_____

Ride Reflection

DATE: / /
HORSE: _____

HOW I FELT AT THE START (CIRCLE ONE)

1   2   3   4   5

1 (Very Anxious / Unsure)   5 (Calm & Confident)

TODAYS FOCUS:
_____
_____

SMALL WINS FROM TODAY?   .
_____
_____
_____

SOMETHING I'D LIKE TO GROW/PRACTISE
_____
_____
_____
_____
_____

HOW I FELT AT THE END (CIRCLE ONE)
1   2   3   4   5

A KIND NOTE TO MYSELF
_____
_____
_____

Ride Reflection

DATE: / /
HORSE: _____

HOW I FELT AT THE START (CIRCLE ONE)

1   2   3   4   5

1 (Very Anxious / Unsure)   5 (Calm & Confident)

TODAYS FOCUS:
_____
_____

SMALL WINS FROM TODAY?   .
_____
_____
_____

SOMETHING I'D LIKE TO GROW/PRACTISE
_____
_____
_____
_____
_____

HOW I FELT AT THE END (CIRCLE ONE)
1   2   3   4   5

A KIND NOTE TO MYSELF
_____
_____
_____

Ride Reflection

DATE: / /

HORSE: _____

HOW I FELT AT THE START (CIRCLE ONE)

1   2   3   4   5

1 (Very Anxious / Unsure)   5 (Calm & Confident)

TODAYS FOCUS:
_____
_____

SMALL WINS FROM TODAY?
_____
_____
_____

SOMETHING I'D LIKE TO GROW/PRACTISE
_____
_____
_____
_____

HOW I FELT AT THE END (CIRCLE ONE)

1   2   3   4   5

A KIND NOTE TO MYSELF
_____
_____
_____

Ride Reflection

DATE: / /

HORSE: _____

HOW I FELT AT THE START (CIRCLE ONE)

1   2   3   4   5

1 (Very Anxious / Unsure)   5 (Calm & Confident)

TODAYS FOCUS:
_____
_____

SMALL WINS FROM TODAY?
_____
_____
_____

SOMETHING I'D LIKE TO GROW/PRACTISE
_____
_____
_____
_____

HOW I FELT AT THE END (CIRCLE ONE)

1   2   3   4   5

A KIND NOTE TO MYSELF
_____
_____
_____

Ride Reflection

DATE: / /

HORSE: _____

HOW I FELT AT THE START (CIRCLE ONE)

1   2   3   4   5

1 (Very Anxious / Unsure)   5 (Calm & Confident)

TODAYS FOCUS:
_____
_____

SMALL WINS FROM TODAY? .
_____
_____
_____

SOMETHING I'D LIKE TO GROW/PRACTISE
_____
_____
_____
_____

HOW I FELT AT THE END (CIRCLE ONE)

1   2   3   4   5

A KIND NOTE TO MYSELF
_____
_____
_____

Ride Reflection

DATE: / /

HORSE: _____

HOW I FELT AT THE START (CIRCLE ONE)

1   2   3   4   5

1 (Very Anxious / Unsure)   5 (Calm & Confident)

TODAYS FOCUS:
_____
_____

SMALL WINS FROM TODAY? .
_____
_____
_____

SOMETHING I'D LIKE TO GROW/PRACTISE
_____
_____
_____
_____

HOW I FELT AT THE END (CIRCLE ONE)

1   2   3   4   5

A KIND NOTE TO MYSELF
_____
_____
_____

Ride Reflection

DATE: / /

HORSE: _____

HOW I FELT AT THE START (CIRCLE ONE)

1   2   3   4   5

1 (Very Anxious / Unsure)   5 (Calm & Confident)

TODAYS FOCUS:
_____
_____

SMALL WINS FROM TODAY? .
_____
_____
_____

SOMETHING I'D LIKE TO GROW/PRACTISE
_____
_____
_____
_____
_____

HOW I FELT AT THE END (CIRCLE ONE)

1   2   3   4   5

A KIND NOTE TO MYSELF
_____
_____
_____

Ride Reflection

DATE: / /

HORSE: _____

HOW I FELT AT THE START (CIRCLE ONE)

1   2   3   4   5

1 (Very Anxious / Unsure)   5 (Calm & Confident)

TODAYS FOCUS:
_____
_____

SMALL WINS FROM TODAY? .
_____
_____
_____

SOMETHING I'D LIKE TO GROW/PRACTISE
_____
_____
_____
_____
_____

HOW I FELT AT THE END (CIRCLE ONE)

1   2   3   4   5

A KIND NOTE TO MYSELF
_____
_____
_____

Ride Reflection

DATE: / /
HORSE: _____

HOW I FELT AT THE START (CIRCLE ONE)

1   2   3   4   5

1 (Very Anxious / Unsure)   5 (Calm & Confident)

TODAYS FOCUS:
_____
_____

SMALL WINS FROM TODAY? .
_____
_____
_____

SOMETHING I'D LIKE TO GROW/PRACTISE
_____
_____
_____
_____

HOW I FELT AT THE END (CIRCLE ONE)

1   2   3   4   5

A KIND NOTE TO MYSELF
_____
_____
_____

Ride Reflection

DATE: / /
HORSE: _____

HOW I FELT AT THE START (CIRCLE ONE)

1   2   3   4   5

1 (Very Anxious / Unsure)   5 (Calm & Confident)

TODAYS FOCUS:
_____
_____

SMALL WINS FROM TODAY? .
_____
_____
_____

SOMETHING I'D LIKE TO GROW/PRACTISE
_____
_____
_____
_____

HOW I FELT AT THE END (CIRCLE ONE)

1   2   3   4   5

A KIND NOTE TO MYSELF
_____
_____
_____

Ride Reflection

DATE: / /

HORSE: _____

HOW I FELT AT THE START (CIRCLE ONE)

1   2   3   4   5

1 (Very Anxious / Unsure)   5 (Calm & Confident)

TODAYS FOCUS:

_____
_____

SMALL WINS FROM TODAY? .

_____
_____
_____

SOMETHING I'D LIKE TO GROW/PRACTISE

_____
_____
_____
_____

HOW I FELT AT THE END (CIRCLE ONE)

1   2   3   4   5

A KIND NOTE TO MYSELF

_____
_____
_____

Ride Reflection

DATE: / /

HORSE: _____

HOW I FELT AT THE START (CIRCLE ONE)

1   2   3   4   5

1 (Very Anxious / Unsure)   5 (Calm & Confident)

TODAYS FOCUS:

_____
_____

SMALL WINS FROM TODAY? .

_____
_____
_____

SOMETHING I'D LIKE TO GROW/PRACTISE

_____
_____
_____
_____

HOW I FELT AT THE END (CIRCLE ONE)

1   2   3   4   5

A KIND NOTE TO MYSELF

_____
_____
_____

Ride Reflection

DATE: / /

HORSE: _____

HOW I FELT AT THE START (CIRCLE ONE)

1   2   3   4   5

1 (Very Anxious / Unsure)   5 (Calm & Confident)

TODAYS FOCUS:
_____
_____

SMALL WINS FROM TODAY? .
_____
_____
_____

SOMETHING I'D LIKE TO GROW/PRACTISE
_____
_____
_____
_____
_____

HOW I FELT AT THE END (CIRCLE ONE)

1   2   3   4   5

A KIND NOTE TO MYSELF
_____
_____
_____

Ride Reflection

DATE: / /

HORSE: _____

HOW I FELT AT THE START (CIRCLE ONE)

1   2   3   4   5

1 (Very Anxious / Unsure)   5 (Calm & Confident)

TODAYS FOCUS:
_____
_____

SMALL WINS FROM TODAY? .
_____
_____
_____

SOMETHING I'D LIKE TO GROW/PRACTISE
_____
_____
_____
_____
_____

HOW I FELT AT THE END (CIRCLE ONE)

1   2   3   4   5

A KIND NOTE TO MYSELF
_____
_____
_____

Ride Reflection

DATE: / /

HORSE: _____

HOW I FELT AT THE START (CIRCLE ONE)

1   2   3   4   5

1 (Very Anxious / Unsure)   5 (Calm & Confident)

TODAYS FOCUS:
_____
_____

SMALL WINS FROM TODAY? .
_____
_____
_____

SOMETHING I'D LIKE TO GROW/PRACTISE
_____
_____
_____
_____

HOW I FELT AT THE END (CIRCLE ONE)

1   2   3   4   5

A KIND NOTE TO MYSELF
_____
_____
_____

Ride Reflection

DATE: / /

HORSE: _____

HOW I FELT AT THE START (CIRCLE ONE)

1   2   3   4   5

1 (Very Anxious / Unsure)   5 (Calm & Confident)

TODAYS FOCUS:
_____
_____

SMALL WINS FROM TODAY? .
_____
_____
_____

SOMETHING I'D LIKE TO GROW/PRACTISE
_____
_____
_____
_____

HOW I FELT AT THE END (CIRCLE ONE)

1   2   3   4   5

A KIND NOTE TO MYSELF
_____
_____
_____

Ride Reflection

DATE: / /

HORSE: _____

HOW I FELT AT THE START (CIRCLE ONE)

1   2   3   4   5

1 (Very Anxious / Unsure)   5 (Calm & Confident)

TODAYS FOCUS:
_____
_____

SMALL WINS FROM TODAY? .
_____
_____
_____

SOMETHING I'D LIKE TO GROW/PRACTISE
_____
_____
_____
_____

HOW I FELT AT THE END (CIRCLE ONE)

1   2   3   4   5

A KIND NOTE TO MYSELF
_____
_____
_____

Ride Reflection

DATE: / /

HORSE: _____

HOW I FELT AT THE START (CIRCLE ONE)

1   2   3   4   5

1 (Very Anxious / Unsure)   5 (Calm & Confident)

TODAYS FOCUS:
_____
_____

SMALL WINS FROM TODAY? .
_____
_____
_____

SOMETHING I'D LIKE TO GROW/PRACTISE
_____
_____
_____
_____

HOW I FELT AT THE END (CIRCLE ONE)

1   2   3   4   5

A KIND NOTE TO MYSELF
_____
_____
_____

Ride Reflection

DATE: / /

HORSE: _____

HOW I FELT AT THE START (CIRCLE ONE)

1   2   3   4   5

1 (Very Anxious / Unsure)   5 (Calm & Confident)

TODAYS FOCUS:
_____
_____

SMALL WINS FROM TODAY? .
_____
_____
_____

SOMETHING I'D LIKE TO GROW/PRACTISE
_____
_____
_____
_____

HOW I FELT AT THE END (CIRCLE ONE)

1   2   3   4   5

A KIND NOTE TO MYSELF
_____
_____
_____

Ride Reflection

DATE: / /

HORSE: _____

HOW I FELT AT THE START (CIRCLE ONE)

1   2   3   4   5

1 (Very Anxious / Unsure)   5 (Calm & Confident)

TODAYS FOCUS:
_____
_____

SMALL WINS FROM TODAY? .
_____
_____
_____

SOMETHING I'D LIKE TO GROW/PRACTISE
_____
_____
_____
_____

HOW I FELT AT THE END (CIRCLE ONE)

1   2   3   4   5

A KIND NOTE TO MYSELF
_____
_____
_____

Ride Reflection

DATE: / /

HORSE: _____

HOW I FELT AT THE START (CIRCLE ONE)

1   2   3   4   5

1 (Very Anxious / Unsure)   5 (Calm & Confident)

TODAYS FOCUS:
_____
_____

SMALL WINS FROM TODAY? .
_____
_____
_____

SOMETHING I'D LIKE TO GROW/PRACTISE
_____
_____
_____
_____

HOW I FELT AT THE END (CIRCLE ONE)

1   2   3   4   5

A KIND NOTE TO MYSELF
_____
_____
_____

Ride Reflection

DATE: / /

HORSE: _____

HOW I FELT AT THE START (CIRCLE ONE)

1   2   3   4   5

1 (Very Anxious / Unsure)   5 (Calm & Confident)

TODAYS FOCUS:
_____
_____

SMALL WINS FROM TODAY? .
_____
_____
_____

SOMETHING I'D LIKE TO GROW/PRACTISE
_____
_____
_____
_____

HOW I FELT AT THE END (CIRCLE ONE)

1   2   3   4   5

A KIND NOTE TO MYSELF
_____
_____
_____

Ride Reflection

DATE: / /

HORSE: _____

HOW I FELT AT THE START (CIRCLE ONE)

1 2 3 4 5

1 (Very Anxious / Unsure)   5 (Calm & Confident)

TODAYS FOCUS:
_____
_____

SMALL WINS FROM TODAY? .
_____
_____
_____

SOMETHING I'D LIKE TO GROW/PRACTISE
_____
_____
_____
_____
_____

HOW I FELT AT THE END (CIRCLE ONE)

1 2 3 4 5

A KIND NOTE TO MYSELF
_____
_____
_____

Ride Reflection

DATE: / /

HORSE: _____

HOW I FELT AT THE START (CIRCLE ONE)

1 2 3 4 5

1 (Very Anxious / Unsure)   5 (Calm & Confident)

TODAYS FOCUS:
_____
_____

SMALL WINS FROM TODAY? .
_____
_____
_____

SOMETHING I'D LIKE TO GROW/PRACTISE
_____
_____
_____
_____
_____

HOW I FELT AT THE END (CIRCLE ONE)

1 2 3 4 5

A KIND NOTE TO MYSELF
_____
_____
_____

Ride Reflection

DATE: / /

HORSE: _____

HOW I FELT AT THE START (CIRCLE ONE)

1   2   3   4   5

1 (Very Anxious / Unsure)   5 (Calm & Confident)

TODAYS FOCUS:
_____
_____

SMALL WINS FROM TODAY? .
_____
_____
_____

SOMETHING I'D LIKE TO GROW/PRACTISE
_____
_____
_____
_____

HOW I FELT AT THE END (CIRCLE ONE)

1   2   3   4   5

A KIND NOTE TO MYSELF
_____
_____
_____

Ride Reflection

DATE: / /

HORSE: _____

HOW I FELT AT THE START (CIRCLE ONE)

1   2   3   4   5

1 (Very Anxious / Unsure)   5 (Calm & Confident)

TODAYS FOCUS:
_____
_____

SMALL WINS FROM TODAY? .
_____
_____
_____

SOMETHING I'D LIKE TO GROW/PRACTISE
_____
_____
_____
_____

HOW I FELT AT THE END (CIRCLE ONE)

1   2   3   4   5

A KIND NOTE TO MYSELF
_____
_____
_____

Ride Reflection

DATE: / /

HORSE: _____

HOW I FELT AT THE START (CIRCLE ONE)

1   2   3   4   5

1 (Very Anxious / Unsure)   5 (Calm & Confident)

TODAYS FOCUS:
_____
_____

SMALL WINS FROM TODAY?
_____
_____
_____

SOMETHING I'D LIKE TO GROW/PRACTISE
_____
_____
_____
_____

HOW I FELT AT THE END (CIRCLE ONE)

1   2   3   4   5

A KIND NOTE TO MYSELF
_____
_____
_____

Ride Reflection

DATE: / /

HORSE: _____

HOW I FELT AT THE START (CIRCLE ONE)

1   2   3   4   5

1 (Very Anxious / Unsure)   5 (Calm & Confident)

TODAYS FOCUS:
_____
_____

SMALL WINS FROM TODAY?
_____
_____
_____

SOMETHING I'D LIKE TO GROW/PRACTISE
_____
_____
_____
_____

HOW I FELT AT THE END (CIRCLE ONE)

1   2   3   4   5

A KIND NOTE TO MYSELF
_____
_____
_____

Ride Reflection

DATE: / /
HORSE: _____

HOW I FELT AT THE START (CIRCLE ONE)

1   2   3   4   5

1 (Very Anxious / Unsure)   5 (Calm & Confident)

TODAYS FOCUS:
_____
_____

SMALL WINS FROM TODAY?   .
_____
_____
_____

SOMETHING I'D LIKE TO GROW/PRACTISE
_____
_____
_____
_____

HOW I FELT AT THE END (CIRCLE ONE)

1   2   3   4   5

A KIND NOTE TO MYSELF
_____
_____
_____

Ride Reflection

DATE: / /
HORSE: _____

HOW I FELT AT THE START (CIRCLE ONE)

1   2   3   4   5

1 (Very Anxious / Unsure)   5 (Calm & Confident)

TODAYS FOCUS:
_____
_____

SMALL WINS FROM TODAY?   .
_____
_____
_____

SOMETHING I'D LIKE TO GROW/PRACTISE
_____
_____
_____
_____

HOW I FELT AT THE END (CIRCLE ONE)

1   2   3   4   5

A KIND NOTE TO MYSELF
_____
_____
_____

Ride Reflection

DATE: / /

HORSE: _____

HOW I FELT AT THE START (CIRCLE ONE)

1   2   3   4   5

1 (Very Anxious / Unsure)   5 (Calm & Confident)

TODAYS FOCUS:

_____

_____

SMALL WINS FROM TODAY? .

_____

_____

_____

SOMETHING I'D LIKE TO GROW/PRACTISE

_____

_____

_____

_____

HOW I FELT AT THE END (CIRCLE ONE)

1   2   3   4   5

A KIND NOTE TO MYSELF

_____

_____

_____

Ride Reflection

DATE: / /

HORSE: _____

HOW I FELT AT THE START (CIRCLE ONE)

1   2   3   4   5

1 (Very Anxious / Unsure)   5 (Calm & Confident)

TODAYS FOCUS:

_____

_____

SMALL WINS FROM TODAY? .

_____

_____

_____

SOMETHING I'D LIKE TO GROW/PRACTISE

_____

_____

_____

_____

HOW I FELT AT THE END (CIRCLE ONE)

1   2   3   4   5

A KIND NOTE TO MYSELF

_____

_____

_____

Ride Reflection

DATE: / /

HORSE: _____

HOW I FELT AT THE START (CIRCLE ONE)

1   2   3   4   5

1 (Very Anxious / Unsure)   5 (Calm & Confident)

TODAYS FOCUS:
_____
_____

SMALL WINS FROM TODAY?   .
_____
_____
_____

SOMETHING I'D LIKE TO GROW/PRACTISE
_____
_____
_____
_____

HOW I FELT AT THE END (CIRCLE ONE)

1   2   3   4   5

A KIND NOTE TO MYSELF
_____
_____
_____

Ride Reflection

DATE: / /

HORSE: _____

HOW I FELT AT THE START (CIRCLE ONE)

1   2   3   4   5

1 (Very Anxious / Unsure)   5 (Calm & Confident)

TODAYS FOCUS:
_____
_____

SMALL WINS FROM TODAY?   .
_____
_____
_____

SOMETHING I'D LIKE TO GROW/PRACTISE
_____
_____
_____
_____

HOW I FELT AT THE END (CIRCLE ONE)

1   2   3   4   5

A KIND NOTE TO MYSELF
_____
_____
_____

Ride Reflection

DATE: / /
HORSE: _____

HOW I FELT AT THE START (CIRCLE ONE)

1   2   3   4   5

1 (Very Anxious / Unsure)   5 (Calm & Confident)

TODAYS FOCUS:
_____
_____

SMALL WINS FROM TODAY? .
_____
_____
_____

SOMETHING I'D LIKE TO GROW/PRACTISE
_____
_____
_____
_____

HOW I FELT AT THE END (CIRCLE ONE)

1   2   3   4   5

A KIND NOTE TO MYSELF
_____
_____
_____

Ride Reflection

DATE: / /
HORSE: _____

HOW I FELT AT THE START (CIRCLE ONE)

1   2   3   4   5

1 (Very Anxious / Unsure)   5 (Calm & Confident)

TODAYS FOCUS:
_____
_____

SMALL WINS FROM TODAY? .
_____
_____
_____

SOMETHING I'D LIKE TO GROW/PRACTISE
_____
_____
_____
_____

HOW I FELT AT THE END (CIRCLE ONE)

1   2   3   4   5

A KIND NOTE TO MYSELF
_____
_____
_____

Ride Reflection

DATE: / /

HORSE: _____

HOW I FELT AT THE START (CIRCLE ONE)

1 2 3 4 5

1 (Very Anxious / Unsure)   5 (Calm & Confident)

TODAYS FOCUS:
_____
_____

SMALL WINS FROM TODAY? .
_____
_____
_____

SOMETHING I'D LIKE TO GROW/PRACTISE
_____
_____
_____
_____
_____

HOW I FELT AT THE END (CIRCLE ONE)

1 2 3 4 5

A KIND NOTE TO MYSELF
_____
_____
_____

Ride Reflection

DATE: / /

HORSE: _____

HOW I FELT AT THE START (CIRCLE ONE)

1 2 3 4 5

1 (Very Anxious / Unsure)   5 (Calm & Confident)

TODAYS FOCUS:
_____
_____

SMALL WINS FROM TODAY? .
_____
_____
_____

SOMETHING I'D LIKE TO GROW/PRACTISE
_____
_____
_____
_____
_____

HOW I FELT AT THE END (CIRCLE ONE)

1 2 3 4 5

A KIND NOTE TO MYSELF
_____
_____
_____

Ride Reflection

DATE: / /

HORSE: _____

HOW I FELT AT THE START (CIRCLE ONE)

1   2   3   4   5

1 (Very Anxious / Unsure)   5 (Calm & Confident)

TODAYS FOCUS:
_____
_____

SMALL WINS FROM TODAY?   .
_____
_____
_____

SOMETHING I'D LIKE TO GROW/PRACTISE
_____
_____
_____
_____

HOW I FELT AT THE END (CIRCLE ONE)

1   2   3   4   5

A KIND NOTE TO MYSELF
_____
_____
_____

Ride Reflection

DATE: / /

HORSE: _____

HOW I FELT AT THE START (CIRCLE ONE)

1   2   3   4   5

1 (Very Anxious / Unsure)   5 (Calm & Confident)

TODAYS FOCUS:
_____
_____

SMALL WINS FROM TODAY?   .
_____
_____
_____

SOMETHING I'D LIKE TO GROW/PRACTISE
_____
_____
_____
_____

HOW I FELT AT THE END (CIRCLE ONE)

1   2   3   4   5

A KIND NOTE TO MYSELF
_____
_____
_____

Ride Reflection

DATE: / /

HORSE: _____

HOW I FELT AT THE START (CIRCLE ONE)

1   2   3   4   5

1 (Very Anxious / Unsure)   5 (Calm & Confident)

TODAYS FOCUS:

_____
_____

SMALL WINS FROM TODAY? .

_____
_____
_____

SOMETHING I'D LIKE TO GROW/PRACTISE

_____
_____
_____
_____

HOW I FELT AT THE END (CIRCLE ONE)

1   2   3   4   5

A KIND NOTE TO MYSELF

_____
_____
_____

Ride Reflection

DATE: / /

HORSE: _____

HOW I FELT AT THE START (CIRCLE ONE)

1   2   3   4   5

1 (Very Anxious / Unsure)   5 (Calm & Confident)

TODAYS FOCUS:

_____
_____

SMALL WINS FROM TODAY? .

_____
_____
_____

SOMETHING I'D LIKE TO GROW/PRACTISE

_____
_____
_____
_____

HOW I FELT AT THE END (CIRCLE ONE)

1   2   3   4   5

A KIND NOTE TO MYSELF

_____
_____
_____

Monthly Progress Check-in

Monthly Progress Check-In

Month _____

MY CONFIDENCE BASELINE THIS MONTH:
Has my comfort Changed?

_____
_____
_____

MY HORSE'S PROGRESS THIS MONTH:

_____
_____
_____

A MOMENT THAT FELT GOOD:

_____
_____
_____

SOMETHING THAT SURPRISED ME (GOOD OR NEUTRAL):

_____
_____
_____

ONE MINDSET INSIGHT I'M TAKING FORWARD:

_____
_____
_____

MINI GOAL FOR NEXT MONTH:

_____
_____

Monthly Progress Check-In

Month _____

MY CONFIDENCE BASELINE THIS MONTH:
Has my comfort Changed?

_____
_____
_____

MY HORSE'S PROGRESS THIS MONTH:

_____
_____
_____

A MOMENT THAT FELT GOOD:

_____
_____
_____

SOMETHING THAT SURPRISED ME (GOOD OR NEUTRAL):

_____
_____
_____

ONE MINDSET INSIGHT I'M TAKING FORWARD:

_____
_____
_____

MINI GOAL FOR NEXT MONTH:

_____
_____

Monthly Progress Check-In

Month _____

MY CONFIDENCE BASELINE THIS MONTH:
Has my comfort Changed?

_____
_____
_____

MY HORSE'S PROGRESS THIS MONTH:

_____
_____
_____

A MOMENT THAT FELT GOOD:

_____
_____
_____

SOMETHING THAT SURPRISED ME (GOOD OR NEUTRAL):

_____
_____
_____

ONE MINDSET INSIGHT I'M TAKING FORWARD:

_____
_____
_____

MINI GOAL FOR NEXT MONTH:

_____
_____

Monthly Progress Check-In

Month _____

MY CONFIDENCE BASELINE THIS MONTH:
Has my comfort Changed?

_____
_____
_____

MY HORSE'S PROGRESS THIS MONTH:

_____
_____
_____

A MOMENT THAT FELT GOOD:

_____
_____
_____

SOMETHING THAT SURPRISED ME (GOOD OR NEUTRAL):

_____
_____
_____

ONE MINDSET INSIGHT I'M TAKING FORWARD:

_____
_____
_____

MINI GOAL FOR NEXT MONTH:

_____
_____

Monthly Progress Check-In

Month _____

MY CONFIDENCE BASELINE THIS MONTH:
Has my comfort Changed?

_____
_____
_____

MY HORSE'S PROGRESS THIS MONTH:

_____
_____
_____

A MOMENT THAT FELT GOOD:

_____
_____
_____

SOMETHING THAT SURPRISED ME (GOOD OR NEUTRAL):

_____
_____

ONE MINDSET INSIGHT I'M TAKING FORWARD:

_____
_____
_____

MINI GOAL FOR NEXT MONTH:

_____
_____

Monthly Progress Check-In

Month _____

MY CONFIDENCE BASELINE THIS MONTH:
Has my comfort Changed?

_____
_____
_____

MY HORSE'S PROGRESS THIS MONTH:

_____
_____
_____

A MOMENT THAT FELT GOOD:

_____
_____
_____

SOMETHING THAT SURPRISED ME (GOOD OR NEUTRAL):

_____
_____
_____

ONE MINDSET INSIGHT I'M TAKING FORWARD:

_____
_____
_____

MINI GOAL FOR NEXT MONTH:

_____
_____

Monthly Progress Check-In

Month _____

MY CONFIDENCE BASELINE THIS MONTH:
Has my comfort Changed?

_____
_____
_____

MY HORSE'S PROGRESS THIS MONTH:

_____
_____
_____

A MOMENT THAT FELT GOOD:

_____
_____
_____

SOMETHING THAT SURPRISED ME (GOOD OR NEUTRAL):

_____
_____
_____

ONE MINDSET INSIGHT I'M TAKING FORWARD:

_____
_____
_____

MINI GOAL FOR NEXT MONTH:

_____
_____

Monthly Progress Check-In

Month _____

MY CONFIDENCE BASELINE THIS MONTH:
Has my comfort Changed?

_____
_____
_____

MY HORSE'S PROGRESS THIS MONTH:

_____
_____
_____

A MOMENT THAT FELT GOOD:

_____
_____
_____

SOMETHING THAT SURPRISED ME (GOOD OR NEUTRAL):

_____
_____
_____

ONE MINDSET INSIGHT I'M TAKING FORWARD:

_____
_____
_____

MINI GOAL FOR NEXT MONTH:

_____
_____

Monthly Progress Check-In

Month _____

MY CONFIDENCE BASELINE THIS MONTH:
Has my comfort Changed?

_____
_____
_____

MY HORSE'S PROGRESS THIS MONTH:

_____
_____
_____

A MOMENT THAT FELT GOOD:

_____
_____
_____

SOMETHING THAT SURPRISED ME (GOOD OR NEUTRAL):

_____
_____
_____

ONE MINDSET INSIGHT I'M TAKING FORWARD:

_____
_____
_____

MINI GOAL FOR NEXT MONTH:

_____
_____

Monthly Progress Check-In

Month _____

MY CONFIDENCE BASELINE THIS MONTH:
Has my comfort Changed?

_____
_____
_____

MY HORSE'S PROGRESS THIS MONTH:

_____
_____
_____

A MOMENT THAT FELT GOOD:

_____
_____
_____

SOMETHING THAT SURPRISED ME (GOOD OR NEUTRAL):

_____
_____
_____

ONE MINDSET INSIGHT I'M TAKING FORWARD:

_____
_____
_____

MINI GOAL FOR NEXT MONTH:

_____
_____

Monthly Progress Check-In

Month _____

MY CONFIDENCE BASELINE THIS MONTH:
Has my comfort Changed?

_____
_____
_____

MY HORSE'S PROGRESS THIS MONTH:

_____
_____
_____

A MOMENT THAT FELT GOOD:

_____
_____
_____

SOMETHING THAT SURPRISED ME (GOOD OR NEUTRAL):

_____
_____
_____

ONE MINDSET INSIGHT I'M TAKING FORWARD:

_____
_____
_____

MINI GOAL FOR NEXT MONTH:

_____
_____

Monthly Progress Check-In

Month _____

MY CONFIDENCE BASELINE THIS MONTH:
Has my comfort Changed?

_____
_____
_____

MY HORSE'S PROGRESS THIS MONTH:

_____
_____
_____

A MOMENT THAT FELT GOOD:

_____
_____
_____

SOMETHING THAT SURPRISED ME (GOOD OR NEUTRAL):

_____
_____
_____

ONE MINDSET INSIGHT I'M TAKING FORWARD:

_____
_____
_____

MINI GOAL FOR NEXT MONTH:

_____
_____

When Fear Spikes (What to Do in the Moment)

- Breathe low, not high in your chest
- Look where you want to go
- Short reins = tense shoulders → soften and lengthen
- Say (out loud, if needed):
- "I am allowed to take my time."
- "I don't have to be perfect to be improving."

Quick Grounding Exercise:
1. Pause.
2. Feel your seat bones.
3. Exhale slowly through your mouth.
4. Let your horse's walk swing your hips.
5. Name 3 things you did right today.

Confidence
Anchor Phrases

> PROGRESS IS PROGRESS, EVEN WHEN IT'S QUIET.

> I AM ALLOWED TO TAKE THIS AT MY PACE.

> MY HORSE AND I ARE LEARNING TOGETHER.

> BRAVERY IS SHOWING UP, NOT ELIMINATING FEAR.

> I CAN BREATHE AND SOFTEN, EVEN WHEN I'M UNSURE.

www.ingramcontent.com/pod-product-compliance
Lightning Source LLC
Chambersburg PA
CBHW052050070526
44584CB00017B/2118